Liturgy Documentary Series 10

Sunday Celebrations in the Absence of a Priest

United States Catholic Conference
Washington, D.C.

In its 1996 planning document, as approved by the general membership of the National Conference of Catholic Bishops in November 1995, the Secretariat of the Bishops' Committee on the Liturgy was authorized to prepare a volume in the Liturgy Documentary Series on Sunday celebrations in the absence of a priest. *Liturgy Documentary Series, Volume 10: Sunday Celebrations in the Absence of a Priest* was approved by Bishop Donald W. Trautman, chairman of the committee, and authorized for publication by the undersigned.

Reverend Monsignor Dennis M. Schnurr
General Secretary
NCCB/USCC

ISBN 1-57455-105-1

CONTENTS

FOREWORD

The *Constitution on the Sacred Liturgy* promulgated by the Second Vatican Council affirmed the foundational role of the Sunday eucharist in the lives of the faithful:

> By a tradition handed down from the apostles and having its origin from the very day of Christ's resurrection, the Church celebrates the paschal mystery every eighth day, which, with good reason, bears the name of Lord's Day or Sunday. For on this day Christ's faithful must gather together so that, by hearing the word of God and taking part in the eucharist, they may call to mind the passion, the resurrection, and the glorification of the Lord Jesus and may thank God, who "has begotten them again unto a living hope through the resurrection of Jesus Christ from the dead" (1 Peter 1:3). Hence, the Lord's Day is the first holyday of all and should be proposed to the devotion of the faithful and taught to them in such a way that it may become in fact a day of joy and of freedom from work. (*Constitution on the Sacred Liturgy* [SC], no. 106)

The Council Fathers recognized, however, that in some places celebration of the Sunday eucharist might not always be possible and recommended services of the Word in such cases (SC, no. 35.4). Similar provision was made in the 1983 *Code of Canon Law* (canon 1248).

In June 1988, due to the need for such celebrations and arising from requests from conferences of bishops for guidelines to structure these gatherings, the Congregation for Divine Worship issued a *Directory for Sunday Celebrations in the Absence of a Priest*. This directory, while reaffirming the value and significance of the Sunday eucharist, established guidelines for Sunday gatherings in those places where the eucharist cannot be celebrated. This was done so that parish communities might continue to gather and keep Sunday holy, even when they cannot participate in the eucharistic sacrifice.

In 1991, the National Conference of Catholic Bishops approved a statement prepared by the Committee on the Liturgy on Sunday worship in the absence of a priest entitled *Gathered in Steadfast Faith*. While expressing grave concern about the implications of these celebrations, the statement provided guidelines for structuring the celebrations, selecting and training the leaders of worship, and catechizing the faithful who participate. To assist those responsible for preparing these celebrations, the

Committee on the Liturgy published in 1994 a bilingual edition of *Sunday Celebrations in the Absence of a Priest: Leader's Edition*. This ritual book provides the texts needed by a deacon or layperson to lead such celebrations.

This tenth volume of the *Liturgy Documentary Series* includes the complete texts of both the *Directory for Sunday Celebrations in the Absence of a Priest* and *Gathered in Steadfast Faith*, as well as the introduction to *Sunday Celebrations in the Absence of a Priest: Leader's Edition*. It is the hope of the Bishops' Committee on the Liturgy and its Secretariat that this volume will prove useful to those who lead Sunday celebrations in the absence of a priest and to those responsible for their formation. Given current pastoral needs,

> the Bishops' Committee on the Liturgy is convinced that in the present circumstances providing Sunday celebrations under the leadership of a deacon or designated layperson is the best response to the phenomenon of the "priestless Sunday." These celebrations enable communities gathered in steadfast faith to hear and respond to God's Word, to be strengthened and nourished by the body and blood of Christ, and to continue to do the work of Christ in the world. However, it remains for the entire Church to continue to work and pray for more laborers for the harvest, more shepherds for the sheep. The Church has faced similar problems in the past and with a faith-filled hope now looks to the future and to the continuing renewal of all the People of God. (*Gathered in Steadfast Faith*, no. 63)

Reverend Monsignor Alan F. Detscher
Executive Director
Secretariat for the Liturgy
Committee on the Liturgy
National Conference of Catholic Bishops

DIRECTORY FOR
SUNDAY CELEBRATIONS
IN THE
ABSENCE OF A PRIEST

DECREE OF THE CONGREGATION FOR DIVINE WORSHIP

Prot. 691/86

The *Directory for Sunday Celebrations in the Absence of a Priest* is a response to the convergence of several factors. The first of these is the fact that it is not everywhere and always possible to have a complete liturgical celebration of Sunday (no. 2). A second factor is the request over the past few years from several conferences of bishops that the Holy See issue guidelines for this de facto situation (no. 7). A third factor is a matter of experience: in the light of the actual situation and its circumstances the Holy See and many bishops in their local Churches have already turned their attention to Sunday celebrations in the absence of a priest. The *Directory* has profited from such experience in regard to its assessment of the advantages and at the same time the possible limitations of the sort of celebration in question.

The fundamental point of the entire *Directory* is to ensure, in the best way possible and in every situation, the Christian celebration of Sunday. This means remembering that the Mass remains the proper way of celebrating Sunday, but also means recognizing the presence of important elements even when Mass cannot be celebrated.

The intent of the present document is not to encourage, much less facilitate, unnecessary or contrived Sunday assemblies without the celebration of the eucharist. The intent rather is simply to guide and to prescribe what should be done when real circumstances require the decision to have Sunday celebrations in the absence of a priest (nos. 21-22).

The first part of the *Directory* is completely devoted to a summary of the meaning of Sunday, and its point of departure is art. 106 of the Constitution on the Liturgy *Sacrosanctum Concilium* (no. 8).

The second part prescribes the conditions necessary for the decision in a diocese to schedule as a regular occurrence Sunday assemblies in the absence of a priest. From a practical and directive point of view this is the most important part of this document. The document envisions the collaboration of the laity in the cases in question; this is an example of responsibilities that parish priests (pastors) can entrust to lay members of their community.

The third part of the *Directory* is a brief description of the rite for Sunday celebrations of the word along with distribution of communion.

As with similar documents, the application of this *Directory* depends on all the bishops, each acting in accord with the situation of his Church; in matters involving norms for an entire region, the application of the *Directory* depends on the conference of bishops.

What matters above all is ensuring that communities involved in the situation in question have the opportunity to gather together on Sunday, and in a way that coincides with the celebration of the liturgical year (no. 36), and that unites such communities with a community that is celebrating the eucharist with their own parish priest (pastor) (no. 42).

As Pope Paul VI (no. 21) and Pope John Paul II (no. 50) have stated, the purpose of all pastoral endeavor concerned with Sunday is that it be celebrated and regarded in accord with Christian tradition.

PREFACE

1.   From the day of Pentecost, after the coming of the Holy Spirit, the Church of Christ has always faithfully come together to celebrate the paschal mystery on the day called "the Lord's Day" in memory of the Lord's resurrection. In the Sunday assembly the Church reads in all the Scriptures those things that concern Christ[1] and celebrates the eucharist as the memorial of the death and resurrection of the Lord until he comes.

2.   But a complete celebration of the Lord's Day is not always possible. There have been and still are many of the faithful for whom "because of the lack of a priest or some other serious reason, participation in the eucharistic celebration is not possible."[2]

3.   In some regions, after their first evangelization, the bishops have put catechists in charge of gathering the faithful together on Sunday and, in the form of a devotional exercise, of leading them in prayer. In such cases the number of Christians grew and they were scattered in so many and such widely separated places that a priest could not reach them every Sunday.

4.   In other places the faithful were completely blocked from gathering on Sunday, either because of the persecution of Christians or because of other severe restrictions of religious freedom. Like the Christians of old, who held fast to the Sunday assembly even in the face of martyrdom,[3] the faithful today, even when deprived of the presence of an ordained minister, also strive to gather on Sunday for prayer either within a family or in small groups.

5.   On other grounds today, namely, the scarcity of priests, in many places not every parish can have its own eucharistic celebration each Sunday. Further, for various social and economic reasons some parishes have many fewer members. As a consequence many priests are assigned to celebrate Mass several times on Sunday in many, widely scattered churches. But this practice is regarded as not always satisfactory either to the parishes lacking their own parish priest (pastor) or to the priests involved.

6.   In some local Churches, then, because of the conditions indicated, the bishops have judged it necessary to arrange for other Sunday celebrations in the absence of a priest, so that in the best way possible the weekly gathering of the faithful can be continued and the Christian tradition regarding Sunday preserved.

It is by no means unusual, particularly in mission territories, for the faithful themselves, aware of the importance of the Lord's Day and with the help of catechists and religious, to gather to listen to the word of God, to pray, and, in some cases, even to receive communion.

7.   The Congregation for Divine Worship has considered these matters, reviewed the documents already published by the Holy See,[4] and acceded to the wishes of the conferences of bishops. Therefore the Congregation regards it as opportune to recall elements of the teaching on the meaning of Sunday, to lay down the conditions for the lawfulness of such celebrations in dioceses, and to provide guidelines for carrying out such celebrations correctly.

It will be the responsibility of the conferences of bishops, as circumstances suggest, to determine these norms in greater detail, to adapt them to the culture and conditions of their people, and to report their decisions to the Apostolic See.

I. SUNDAY AND ITS OBSERVANCE

8.   "By a tradition handed down from the apostles and having its origin from the very day of Christ's resurrection, the Church celebrates the paschal mystery every eighth day, which, with good reason, bears the name of the Lord's Day or Sunday."[5]

9.   Evidence of the gathering of the faithful on the day which the New Testament itself already designates as the Lord's Day[6] appears explicitly in documents of the first and second centuries.[7] Outstanding among such evidence is the testimony of Saint Justin: "On this day which is called Sunday, all who live in the cities or in the country gather together in one place."[8] But the day of gathering for Christians did not coincide with the day of rest in the Greek or Roman calendar and therefore even the gathering on this day was a sign to fellow citizens of the Christians' identity.

10.   From the earliest centuries pastors had never failed to counsel their people on the need to gather together on Sunday. "Because you are Christ's members, do not scatter from the church by not coming together . . . do not neglect your Savior or separate him from his members. Do not shatter or scatter the Body of Christ. . . ."[9] Vatican Council II recalled this teaching in the following words: "On this day Christ's faithful must gather together, so that, by hearing the word of God and taking part in the eucharist, they may call to mind the passion, resurrection, and glorification of the Lord Jesus and may thank God, who 'has begotten them again unto

a living hope through the resurrection of Jesus Christ from the dead'
(1 Peter 1:3)."[10]

11. Saint Ignatius of Antioch pointed out the importance of the Sunday
celebration for the life of the faithful: "Christians no longer observe the
sabbath day, but live according to the Lord's Day, on which our life was
restored through Jesus Christ and his death."[11] In their "sense of the faith"
(*sensus fidelium*) the faithful, now as in the past, have held the Lord's Day
in such high regard that they have never willingly omitted its observance
even in times of persecution or in the midst of cultures alien or hostile to the
Christian faith.

12. The following are the principal requisites for the Sunday assembly of
the faithful.
a. the gathering of the faithful to manifest the Church, not simply on
their own initiative but as called together by God, that is, as the
people of God in their organic structure, presided over by a
priest, who acts in the person of Christ;
b. their instruction in the paschal mystery through the Scriptures
that are proclaimed and that are explained by a priest or deacon;
c. the celebration of the eucharistic sacrifice, by which the paschal
mystery is expressed, and which is carried out by the priest in the
person of Christ and offered in the name of the entire Christian
people.

13. Pastoral efforts should have this aim above all that the sacrifice of the
Mass on Sunday be regarded as the only true actualization of the Lord's
paschal mystery[12] and as the most complete manifestation of the Church:
"Hence the Lord's Day is the first holyday of all and should be proposed to
the devotion of the faithful and taught to them. . . . Other celebrations,
unless they be truly of greatest importance, shall not have precedence over
the Sunday, the foundation and core of the whole liturgical year."[13]

14. Such principles should be set before the faithful and instilled in them
right from the beginning of their Christian formation, in order that they may
willingly fulfill the precept to keep this day holy and may understand why
they are brought together for the celebration of the eucharist by the call of
the Church[14] and not simply by their personal devotion. In this way the
faithful will be led to experience the Lord's Day as a sign of the divine
transcendence over all human works, and not as simply a day off from work;
in virtue of the Sunday assembly they will more deeply perceive themselves
to be members of the Church and will show this outwardly.

15. In the Sunday assembly, as also in the life of the Christian community,
the faithful should find both active participation and a true spirit of

community, as well as the opportunity to be renewed spiritually under the guidance of the Holy Spirit. In this way, too, they will be protected against the attractions of sects that promise relief from the pain of loneliness and a more complete fulfillment of religious aspirations.

16. Finally, pastoral effort should concentrate on measures which have as their purpose "that the Lord's Day becomes in fact a day of joy and of freedom from work."[15] In this way Sunday will stand out in today's culture as a sign of freedom and consequently as a day established for the well-being of the human person, which clearly is a higher value than commerce or industrial production.[16]

17. The word of God, the eucharist, and the ministry of the priest are gifts that the Lord presents to the Church, his Bride, and they are to be received and to be prayed for as divine graces. The Church, which possesses these gifts above all in the Sunday assembly, thanks God for them in that same assembly and awaits the joy of its complete rest in the day of the Lord "before the throne of God and before the Lamb."[17]

II. CONDITIONS FOR HOLDING SUNDAY CELEBRATIONS IN THE ABSENCE OF A PRIEST

18. Whenever and wherever Mass cannot be celebrated on Sunday, the first thing to be ascertained is whether the faithful can go to a church in a place nearby to participate there in the eucharistic mystery. At the present time this solution is to be recommended and to be retained where it is in effect; but it demands that the faithful, rightly imbued with a fuller understanding of the Sunday assembly, respond with good will to a new situation.

19. The aim is that the riches of Sacred Scripture and of the Church's prayer be amply provided to the faithful gathered on Sundays in various ways even apart from Mass. For the faithful should not be deprived of the readings that are read at Mass in the course of a year, nor of the prayers of the liturgical seasons.

20. Among the forms of celebration found in liturgical tradition when Mass is not possible, a celebration of the word of God is particularly recommended,[18] and also its completion, when possible, by eucharistic communion. In this way the faithful can be nourished by both the word of God and the body of Christ. "By hearing the word of God the faithful learn that the marvels it proclaims reach their climax in the paschal mystery, of which the Mass is a sacramental memorial and in which they share by communion."[19] Further, in certain circumstances the Sunday celebration can be combined with the celebration of one or more of the sacraments and especially of the sacramentals and in ways that are suited to the needs of each community.

21. It is imperative that the faithful be taught to see the substitutional character of these celebrations, which should not be regarded as the optimal solution to new difficulties nor as a surrender to mere convenience.[20] Therefore a gathering or assembly of this kind can never be held on a Sunday in places where Mass has already been celebrated or is to be celebrated or was celebrated on the preceding Saturday evening, even if the Mass is celebrated in a different language. Nor is it right to have more than one assembly of this kind on any given Sunday.

22. Any confusion between this kind of assembly and a eucharistic celebration must be carefully avoided. Assemblies of this kind should not take away but rather increase the desire of the faithful to take part in the celebration of the eucharist, and should make them more eager to be present at the celebration of the eucharist.

23. The faithful are to understand that the eucharistic sacrifice cannot take place without a priest and that the eucharistic communion which they may receive in this kind of assembly is closely connected with the sacrifice of the Mass. On that basis the faithful can be shown how necessary it is to pray that God will "give the Church more priests and keep them faithful in their love and service."[21]

24. It belongs to the diocesan bishop, after hearing the council of presbyters, to decide whether Sunday assemblies without the celebration of the eucharist should be held on a regular basis in his diocese. It belongs also to the bishop, after considering the place and persons involved, to set out both general and particular norms for such celebrations. These assemblies are therefore to be conducted only in virtue of their convocation by the bishop and only under the pastoral ministry of the parish priest (pastor).

25. "No Christian community is ever built up unless it has its roots and center in the eucharistic liturgy."[22] Therefore before the bishop decides on having Sunday assemblies without celebration of the eucharist the following, in addition to the status of parishes (see no. 5), should be considered: the possibility of recourse to priests, even religious priests, who are not directly assigned to the care of souls and the frequency of Masses in the various parishes and churches.[23] The preeminence of the celebration of the eucharist, particularly on Sunday, over other pastoral activities is to be respected.

26. Either personally or through his representatives the bishop will, by an appropriate catechesis, instruct the diocesan community on the causes requiring provision of these celebrations, pointing out the seriousness of the issue and urging the community's support and cooperation. The bishop is to appoint a delegate or a special committee to see to it that these celebrations are carried out correctly; he is also to choose those who are to promote these celebrations, and to see to it that these people receive the necessary instruction. But the bishop's concern is always to be that several times a year the faithful involved have the opportunity to participate in the celebration of the eucharist.

27. It is the duty of the parish priest (pastor) to inform the bishop about the opportuneness of such celebrations in his territory, to prepare the faithful for them, to visit them during the week, and at a convenient time to celebrate the sacraments for them, particularly the sacrament of penance. In this way the communities involved will come to realize that their assembly on Sunday is not an assembly "without a priest," but an assembly "in the absence of a priest," or, better still, an assembly "in expectation of a priest."

28. When Mass cannot be celebrated the parish priest (pastor) is to ensure that holy communion be given. He is also to see to it that there is a celebration of the eucharist in due time in each community. The consecrated hosts are to be renewed often and kept in a safe place.

29. As the primary assistants of priests, deacons are called in a special way to lead these Sunday assemblies. Since the deacon has been ordained for the nurture and increase of the people of God, it belongs to him to lead the prayers, to proclaim the gospel, to preach the homily, and to give communion.[24]

30. In the absence of both a priest and a deacon, the parish priest (pastor) is to appoint laypersons, who are to be entrusted with the care of these celebrations, namely, with leading the prayers, with the ministry of the word, and with giving holy communion.

Those to be chosen first by the parish priest (pastor) are readers and acolytes who have been duly instituted for the service of the altar and of the word of God. If there are no such instituted ministers available, other laypersons, both men and women, may be appointed; they can carry out this responsibility in virtue of their baptism and confirmation.[25] Such persons are to be chosen in view of the consistency of their way of life with the Gospel and in the expectation of their being acceptable to the community of the faithful. Appointment is usually to be for a definite time and is to be made known publicly to the community. It is fitting that there be a celebration in which prayers are offered to God on behalf of those appointed.[26]

The parish priest (pastor) is to see to the suitable and continuous instruction of these laypersons and to prepare with them worthy celebrations (see Chapter III).

31. The laypersons appointed should regard the office entrusted to them not so much as an honor but as a responsibility and above all as a service to their brothers and sisters under the authority of the parish priest (pastor). For theirs is not a proper office but a suppletory office, since they exercise it "where the need of the Church suggests in the absence of ministers."[27]

Those who are appointed to such an office "should do all of, but only, those parts which pertain to that office."[28] They should carry out their office with sincere devotion and the decorum demanded by such a responsibility and rightly expected of them by God's people.[29]

32. When on a Sunday a celebration of the word of God along with the giving of holy communion is not possible, the faithful are strongly urged to devote themselves to prayer "for a suitable time either individually or with the family or, if possible, with a group of families."[30] In these circumstances the telecast of liturgical services can provide useful assistance.

33. Particularly to be kept in mind is the possibility of celebrating some part of the liturgy of the hours, for example, morning prayer or evening prayer, during which the Sunday readings of the current year can be inserted. For "when the people are invited to the liturgy of the hours and come together in unity of heart and voice, they show forth the Church in its celebration of the mystery of Christ."[31] At the end of such a celebration communion may be given (see no. 46).

34. "The grace of the Redeemer is not lacking for individual members of the faithful or entire communities that, because of persecution or a lack of priests, are deprived of celebration of the eucharist for a short time or even for a long period. They can be moved by a deep desire for the sacrament and be united in prayer with the whole Church. Then when they call upon the Lord and raise their minds and hearts to him, through the power of the Holy Spirit they enter into communion with Christ and with the Church, his living Body . . . and therefore they receive the fruits of the eucharist."[32]

III. ORDER OF CELEBRATION

35. The order to be followed in a Sunday celebration that does not include Mass consists of two parts, the celebration of the word of God and the giving of holy communion. Nothing that is proper to Mass, and particularly the presentation of the gifts and the eucharistic prayer, is to be inserted into the celebration. The order of celebration is to be arranged in such a way that it is truly conducive to prayer and conveys the image not of a simple meeting but of a genuine liturgical assembly.

36. As a rule the texts for the prayers and readings for each Sunday or solemnity are to be taken from *The Roman Missal (Sacramentary)* and the *Lectionary for Mass*. In this way the faithful will follow the cycle of the liturgical year and will pray and listen to the word of God in communion with the other communities of the Church.

37. In preparing the celebration the parish priest (pastor) together with the appointed laypersons may make adaptations suited to the number of those who will take part in the celebration, the ability of the leaders (animators), and the kind of instruments available for the music and the singing.

38. When a deacon presides at the celebration, he acts in accord with his ministry in regard to the greetings, the prayers, the gospel reading and homily, the giving of communion, and the dismissal and blessing. He wears the vestments proper to his ministry, that is, the alb with stole, and, as circumstances suggest, the dalmatic. He uses the presidential chair.

39. A layperson who leads the assembly acts as one among equals, in the way followed in the liturgy of the hours when not presided over by an ordained minister, and in the case of blessings when the minister is a layperson ("May the Lord bless us. . . ."; "Let us praise the Lord. . . ."). The layperson is not to use words that are proper to a priest or deacon and is to omit rites that are too readily associated with the Mass, for example, greetings—especially "The Lord be with you"—and dismissals, since these might give the impression that the layperson is a sacred minister.[33]

40. The lay leader wears vesture that is suitable for his or her function or the vesture prescribed by the bishop.[34] He or she does not use the presidential chair, but another chair prepared outside the sanctuary.[35] Since the altar is the table of sacrifice and of the paschal banquet, its only use in this celebration is for the rite of communion, when the consecrated bread is placed on it before communion is given.

Preparation of the celebration should include careful attention to a suitable distribution of offices, for example, for the readings, the singing, etc., and also to the arrangement and decoration of the place of celebration.

41. The following is an outline of the elements of the celebration.
    a.   Introductory rites. The purpose of these is to form the gathered

faithful into a community and for them to dispose themselves for the celebration.
b. Liturgy of the word. Here God speaks to his people, to disclose to them the mystery of redemption and salvation; the people respond through the profession of faith and the general intercessions.
c. Thanksgiving. Here God is blessed for his great glory (see no. 45).
d. Communion rites. These are an expression and accomplishment of communion with Christ and with his members, especially with those who on this same day take part in the eucharistic sacrifice.
e. Concluding rites. These point to the connection existing between the liturgy and the Christian life.

The conference of bishops, or the individual bishop himself, may, in view of the conditions of the place and the people involved, determine more precisely the details of the celebration, using resources prepared by the national or diocesan liturgical committee, but the general structure of the celebration should not be changed unnecessarily.

42. In the introduction at the beginning of the celebration, or at some other point, the leader should make mention of the community of the faithful with whom the parish priest (pastor) is celebrating the eucharist on that Sunday and urge the assembly to unite itself in spirit with that community.

43. In order that the participants may retain the word of God, there should be an explanation of the readings or a period of silence for reflection on what has been heard. Since only a priest or a deacon may give a homily,[36] it is desirable that the parish priest (pastor) prepare a homily and give it to the leader of the assembly to be read. But in this matter the decisions of the conference of bishops are to be followed.

44. The general intercessions are to follow an established series of intentions.[37] Intentions for the whole diocese that the bishop may have proposed are not to be omitted. There should also often be intentions for vocations to sacred orders, for the bishop, and for the parish priest (pastor).

45. The thanksgiving may follow either one of the ways described here.
1. After the general intercessions or after holy communion, the leader invites all to an act of thanksgiving, in which the faithful praise the glory and mercy of God. This can be done by use of a psalm (for example, Psalms 100, 113, 118, 136, 147, 150), a hymn (for example, the *Gloria*), a canticle (for example, the Canticle of

Mary), or a litanic prayer. The leader and the faithful, stand, and facing the altar, together recite the thanksgiving.

2. After the Lord's Prayer, the leader of the assembly goes to the tabernacle or other place where the eucharist is reserved and, after making a reverence, places the ciborium with the holy eucharist on the altar. Then while kneeling before the altar he or she together with all the faithful sing or recite a hymn, psalm, or litany, which in this case is directed to Christ in the eucharist.

But this thanksgiving is not in any way to take the form of the eucharistic prayer, the texts of prefaces or eucharistic prayers from *The Roman Missal (Sacramentary)* are not to be used, and all danger of confusion is to be removed.

46. For the communion rite the provisions given in *The Roman Ritual* for communion outside Mass are to be observed.[38] The faithful are to be frequently reminded that even when they receive communion outside Mass they are united to the eucharistic sacrifice.

47. For communion, if at all possible, bread consecrated that same Sunday in a Mass celebrated elsewhere is used; a deacon or layperson brings it in a ciborium or pyx and places it in the tabernacle before the celebration. Bread consecrated at the last Mass celebrated in the place of assembly may also be used. Before the Lord's Prayer the leader goes to the tabernacle or place where the eucharist is reserved, takes the vessel with the body of the Lord, and places it upon the table of the altar, then introduces the Lord's Prayer—unless the act of thanksgiving mentioned in no. 45, 2 is to take place at this point.

48. The Lord's Prayer is always recited or sung by all, even if there is to be no communion. The sign of peace may be exchanged. After communion, "a period of silence may be observed or a psalm or song of praise may be sung."[39] A thanksgiving as described in no. 45, 1 may also take place here.

49. Before the conclusion of the assembly, announcements or notices related to the life of the parish or the diocese are read.

50. "Too much importance can never be attached to the Sunday assembly, whether as the source of the Christian life of the individual and of the community, or as a sign of God's intent to gather the whole human race together in Christ.

"All Christians must share the conviction that they cannot live their faith or participate—in the manner proper to them—in the universal mission of the Church unless they are nourished by the eucharistic bread. They should be equally convinced that the Sunday assembly is a sign to the world of the mystery of communion, which is the eucharist."[40]

On 21 May 1988 this Directory, prepared by the Congregation for Divine Worship, was approved and confirmed by Pope John Paul II, who also ordered its publication.

From the office of the Congregation for Divine Worship, Solemnity of the Body and Blood of Christ, 2 June 1988.

Paul Augustin Cardinal Mayer, O.S.B.
Prefect

+Vergilio Noé
Titular Archbishop of Voncaria
Secretary

NOTES

1. See Luke 24:17.
2. *Codex Iuris Canonici*, 1983 (hereafter, CIC), can. 1248, §2.
3. See *Acta Martyrum Bytiniae*, in D. Ruiz Bueno, *Actas de los Martires*, Biblioteca de Autores Cristianos (BAC) 75 (Madrid, 1951), 973.
4. See SC Rites, Instruction *Inter Oecumenici* (26 September 1964), no. 37: *Acta Apostolicae Sedis* (hereafter, AAS) 56 (1964), 884-885; *Documents on the Liturgy, 1963-1979: Conciliar, Papal, and Curial Texts* (hereafter, DOL) 23, no. 329. CIC, can. 1248, §2.
5. *Vatican Council II,* Constitution on the Liturgy *Sacrosanctum Concilium* (hereafter, SC), art. 106: DOL 1, no. 106. See also ibid., *Appendix, Declaration of the Second Vatican Ecumenical Council on Revision of the Calendar:* DOL 1, no. 131.
6. See Revelation 1:10. See also John 20:19, 26; Acts 20:7-12; 1 Corinthians 16:2; Hebrews 10:24-25.
7. Didache 14, 1: F. X. Funk, ed., *Doctrina duodecim Apostolorum* (1887), 42.
8. Saint Justin, *Apologia* I, 67: PG 6, 430.
9. *Didascalia Apostolorum* 2, 59, 1-3: F. X. Funk, ed., *Didascalia et Constitutiones Apostolorum* (1905) vol. 1, 170.
10. SC, art. 106: DOL 1, no. 106.
11. Saint Ignatius of Antioch, *Ad Magnesios* 9, 1: F. X. Funk ed., *Didascalia et Constitutiones Apostolorum* (1905) vol. 1, 199.
12. See Paul VI, Address to bishops of central France, 26 March 1977: AAS 69 (1977), 465; "The goal must always be the celebration of the sacrifice of the Mass, the only true actualization of the Lord's paschal mystery": DOL 449, no. 38:2.
13. SC, art. 106: DOL 1, no. 106.

14. See SC Rites, Instruction *Eucharisticum mysterium* (25 May 1967), no. 25: AAS 59 (1967), 555; DOL 179, no. 25.

15. SC, art. 106: DOL 1, no. 106.

16. See "Le sens du dimanche dans une societé pluraliste. Reflexions pastorales de la Conference des évêques du Canada," *La Documentation Catholique*, no. 1935 (1987), 273-276.

17. Revelation 7:9.

18. See SC, art. 35, 4: DOL 1, no. 35.

19. *The Roman Ritual, Holy Communion and Worship of the Eucharist Outside Mass*, no. 26.

20. See Paul VI, Address to bishops of Central France, 26 March 1977: AAS 69 (1977); "Proceed judiciously, but without multiplying this type of Sunday assembly, as though it were the ideal solution and the last chance": DOL 449, no. 3842.

21. *The Roman Missal (Sacramentary)*, Masses and Prayers for Various Needs and Occasions, I. For the Church, 9. For Priestly Vocations, prayer over the gifts.

22. Vatican Council II, Decree on the Ministry and Life of Priests *Presbyterorum ordinis*, no. 6: DOL 18, no. 261.

23. See SC Rites, Instruction *Eucharisticum mysterium* (25 May 1967), no. 26: AAS 59 (1967), 555; DOL 179, no. 1255.

24. See Paul VI, Motu proprio *Ad pascendum* (15 August 1972), no. 1: AAS 64 (1972), 534; DOL 319, no. 2576.

25. See CIC, can. 230, §3.

26. See *The Roman Ritual, Book of Blessings*, ch. 4, I, B.

27. CIC, can. 230, §3.

28. SC, art. 28: DOL 1, no. 28.

29. See SC, art. 29: DOL 1, no. 29.

30. CIC, can. 1248, §2.

31. *General Instruction of the Liturgy of the Hours* (hereafter, GILH), no. 22: DOL 426, no. 3452.

32. Congregation for the Doctrine of the Faith, *Epistle . . . on certain questions regarding the minister of the eucharist* (6 August 1983): AAS 75 (1983), 1007.

33. See GILH, no. 258: DOL 426, no. 3688; see also *The Roman Ritual, Book of Blessings*, nos. 48, 119, 130, 181.

34. See *The Roman Ritual, Holy Communion and Worship of the Eucharist Outside Mass*, no. 20: DOL 266, no. 2098.

35. See GILH, no. 258: DOL 426, no. 3688.

36. See CIC, can. 766-767.

37. See *General Instruction of the Roman Missal*, nos. 45-47: DOL 208, nos. 1435-1437.

38. See *The Roman Ritual, Holy Communion and Worship of the Eucharist Outside Mass*, ch. 1: DOL 266. nos. 2092-2103.

39. Ibid., no. 37.

40. John Paul II, Address to the bishops of France on the occasion of their *ad limina* visit, 27 March 1987.

GATHERED IN STEADFAST FAITH

STATEMENT OF THE BISHOPS' COMMITTEE ON THE LITURGY ON SUNDAY WORSHIP IN THE ABSENCE OF A PRIEST

INTRODUCTION

1.   When the Catholic Church was just beginning to take root in North America, it often happened that only on an occasional Sunday could the new communities expect to gather for the celebration of the Mass. Priests found it necessary to divide their presence among a circuit of fledgling parishes. As a result, Catholic families in those communities would stay at home on other Sundays for family devotions, private prayer, festive meals, and the observance of the Sunday rest.

2.   Today an increasing number of Catholic communities throughout the United States are faced with a similar reality: the necessity of observing Sunday, of keeping holy the Lord's Day, without the liturgical leadership of their priest. In many dioceses, large parishes which formerly had several priests may now have only one; parishes which once had a resident pastor are now served by a priest traveling from a nearby community; areas that once had large Catholic populations, e.g., inner cities, are now experiencing population shifts; people are moving to different regions of the country, but they are not bringing clergy with them; some parishes have been and will continue to be combined with neighboring ones.

3.   This situation, while being a serious problem facing the Church, is also a cause for reflection upon the mystery of the Church and the role of all the baptized in its mission. It raises the possibility of creative solutions in the redistribution of ordained priests within and among dioceses and of new approaches in the discernment and nurturing of vocations to the priesthood.

4.   Until such new approaches bear fruit, there will continue to be priests in certain areas of the country who must celebrate Mass several times on Sundays in many widely scattered churches in order to serve the needs of the faithful. These priests are to be commended for their dedication and pastoral zeal.

5.   It is the entire Church which the New Testament refers to as "'a chosen race, a royal priesthood, a holy nation, a people of his own, so that you may announce the praises' of him who called you out of darkness into his wonderful light" (1 Peter 2:9). Through baptism all Christians are called to holiness and are commissioned for Christian service to the Church and to the world. Through baptism all participate in the paschal mystery of the

Lord's dying and rising; all are called to continual conversion, ever-stronger discipleship, abundant life, and unfailing hope.

6.   The common priesthood of all the baptized provides impetus for the Catholic people of God to gather in solemn assembly for worship on the Lord's Day, normally with the celebration of the eucharist. Likewise, when the community of believers is deprived of priests and therefore unable to celebrate the eucharist, the bishop should make provisions that will enable it to assemble on Sunday in order to be strengthened in faith through various liturgical celebrations. Such communities may celebrate Morning or Evening Prayer from the Liturgy of the Hours or have a Celebration of the Liturgy of the Word, all of which may include the distribution of holy communion, reserved for this purpose.

7.   This statement of the Bishops' Committee on the Liturgy acknowledges a growing need for these celebrations. At the same time, the committee wishes to reaffirm the constant teaching of the Church concerning the primacy of Sunday, its intimate connection with the celebration of the eucharist, and the constitutive nature of the ministerial priesthood for the life of the Church. The statement affirms that the Church is by its nature sacramental, and that the full eucharistic celebration is the fount and summit of the life of the Church.[1] It also addresses the many modes of Christ's presence in the community, the Sunday assembly as a visible gathering of the Church, and the need for well-prepared and reverently celebrated liturgical prayer.

8.   In addition, this statement presents several points for the consideration of those communities which, because of the absence of priests, are unable to have the celebration of Mass on Sunday. It recognizes that alternative liturgical celebrations cannot truly substitute for the eucharistic sacrifice, for it is in the eucharistic celebration that "the entire Church recognizes and gives expression to itself."[2] But when necessity demands that the Sunday liturgy take another form, it is to be structured in the best way possible while being made clear to all that it is not the Mass. In addition, assemblies without the presence of a priest are to be encouraged to look forward to the celebration of the eucharist; one way of helping to ensure this is through good celebrations of other forms of liturgical prayer until such assemblies may once again celebrate the eucharist each Sunday.

9.   This statement has been prepared in light of the *Directory for Sunday Celebrations in the Absence of a Priest*, issued by the Congregation for Divine Worship on 2 June 1988. It is meant to assist diocesan bishops, who are faced with the unavoidable reality of Sunday assemblies deprived of the celebration of Mass. The statement is seen as providing for a present need,

while never forgetting the plea of the Good Shepherd, "Ask the master of the harvest to send out laborers for his harvest" (Matthew 9:38; Luke 10:2).

I. THE TRADITION
OF SUNDAY,
THE DAY OF THE LORD

10.　From its earliest days the Christian faithful have assembled for corporate worship on the Lord's Day. It was on the "first day of the week," according to the Jewish calendar, that Christ rose from the dead and appeared to and was present with his disciples (see Matthew 28:1, Mark 16:2, Luke 24:1, John 20:1). No doubt it was for this reason that Christ's followers met on the first day of each week for common and, almost certainly, eucharistic worship. Saint Paul presumed this weekly gathering of the Church (1 Corinthians 16:2).

11.　For Christians the earliest term for Sunday was "the first day of the week." That was soon replaced by "the Lord's Day" (see Revelation 1:10; Ignatius, *Letter to the Magnesians* 9:1; *Didache* 14:1), a term which was used along side of the customary civil designation of "the day named after the sun," that is, "Sunday." In about 150 A.D. Justin Martyr wrote concerning the activity on this day:

> And on the day called Sunday there is a meeting in one place of those who live in cities or the country, and the memoirs of the apostles or the writings of the prophets are read as long as time permits. . . . Then we all stand up together and offer prayers. And, as said before, when we have finished the prayer, bread is brought, and wine and water, and the president similarly sends up prayers and thanksgivings to the best of his ability, and the congregation assents, saying the Amen; the distribution, and reception of the consecrated (elements) by each one, takes place and they are sent to the absent by the deacons. . . . We all hold this common gathering on Sunday, since it is the first day, on which God transforming darkness and matter made the universe, and Jesus Christ our Savior rose from the dead on the same day.[3]

12.　Keeping the Lord's Day by coming together for the weekly assembly was regarded as essential in the life of a Christian, even in times of persecution: "We have to celebrate the Lord's Day. It is our rule. . . . We could not live without celebrating the Lord's Day," the martyrs of Abitina asserted.[4]

20

13. For Christians Sunday was always a day of joy;[5] no one was allowed to fast[6] or to kneel.[7] It became a day of rest after 321 A.D. when Constantine closed the law courts and stopped people from working on that day. Under Constantine Sunday became the Christian festival of the Roman Empire.

14. In their observance of the Lord's Day the early Christians realized their identity and mission. In their eucharistic celebrations they strengthened their faith, steadied themselves for further worship and service in society, helped to liberate themselves from the manifold pressures of an isolating and alienating existence, and readied themselves again to become more clearly the life and the leaven of the world.[8]

15. This weekly celebration of Christians remains as a "sign" of the salvific reality of the new creation that began with the resurrection of Christ. As a feast of the Christian assembly, a day of eucharistic celebration, and a day of Christian anticipation of what is to come, Sunday is indispensable, and no other day of the week can be substituted for it.[9]

II. SUNDAY, THE PREEMINENT DAY FOR THE EUCHARIST

16. Whenever the Christian community gathers to celebrate the eucharist, it shows forth the death and resurrection of the Lord in the hope of his glorious coming.[10] "In the Mass we have the high point of the work that in Christ God accomplishes to sanctify us and the high point of the worship that in adoring God through Christ, his Son, we offer to the Father."[11] By entering into the eucharistic action, the community enters into the sharing of the body and blood of Christ, for "the sharing of the body and blood of Christ does nothing less than transform us into what we receive."[12] By sharing in the eucharistic body and blood of Christ, the Church becomes the body of Christ in the world, and by being united to Christ, the head of the Church, the members of his body are united to one another.

17. Saint John Chrysostom, when speaking of the central importance of the eucharist in the life of the Christian, declared, "To abstain from this meal is to separate oneself from the Lord: the Sunday meal is that which we take in common with the Lord and with the brothers and sisters."[13] The eucharist, then, is a celebration of communion, of union with the Lord Jesus and with his Body, the Church, that unites and transforms both the individual and the community.

III. SUNDAY CELEBRATIONS WHEN A PRIEST CANNOT BE PRESENT

18. When a priest cannot be present for the celebration of Mass on the Lord's Day, it is of paramount importance that the parish or mission community still come together to celebrate the resurrection of the Lord.[14] If in the judgment of the diocesan bishop it is not practical or possible for the community to participate in the celebration of Mass in a church nearby,[15] they should assemble for Sunday worship in their own community under the leadership of the person the bishop, in consultation with the pastor, has designated to lead them in prayer. In such a case the celebration may take one of the forms given in the *Sunday Celebrations in the Absence of a Priest: Leader's Edition*: Morning or Evening Prayer or a Celebration of the Liturgy of the Word, all of which may include the distribution of holy communion.

19. By continuing to gather on the Lord's Day to hear God's word and reflect on it, to make intercession for the Church and the world, to sing God's praises, and to encourage one another in the life of grace,[16] the community expresses and develops itself as Church. It contributes to the building up of the faith of its members; it gives glory to God.

20. The faith of a Catholic Christian is normally lived in the context of a parish community; for it is there that faith is nourished and celebrated. Thus, even when the Sunday eucharist is not available, the community's gathering for worship preserves the sanctity of the Lord's Day, helps them to remain in the habit of assembling on Sunday, and prepares them for the time when there will be a priest to lead the community in the Sunday eucharist.[17] These Sunday assemblies also provide opportunities within the community for nurturing vocations to the priesthood and diaconate and for continual prayer for vocations to the ordained ministries of the Church.

21. These Sunday celebrations will also contribute to the preservation of programs of catechetical instruction, the care of the sick and of persons with disabilities, and small gatherings for study, prayer and witness in the community. The community is less likely to grow in faith—or even sustain its faith—if the Sunday liturgical assembly disperses in various directions. Therefore, no effort should be spared in helping foster the celebration of faith, particularly on Sunday—even in the absence of a priest in those ecclesial communities judged by the bishop to be viable, independent faith communities.

22. The thought of Roman Catholics gathering for Sunday worship without the celebration of the Mass is altogether new for most. The years of liturgical renewal since the Second Vatican Council have rightly reinforced the understanding that the eucharist is both essential and central to the lives of the faithful. For it is in the eucharistic action that the Church encounters Christ in a preeminent way and through a variety of modes:

> First, he is present in the very assembly of the faithful, gathered together in his name; next, he is present in his word, with the reading and explanation of Scripture in the church; also in the person of the minister; finally, and above all, in the eucharistic elements. In a way that is completely unique, the whole and entire Christ, God and man, is substantially and permanently present in the sacrament. This presence of Christ under the appearance of bread and wine "is called real, not to exclude other kinds of presence as though they were not real, but because it is real par excellence."[18]

Yet throughout the ages Christians have believed that Christ is present in other liturgical celebrations in the ways indicated above.

23. Divine Revelation continually underscores the Church's understanding that Christ is present in the assembly of the faithful,[19] especially when it gathers in prayer.[20] Christ manifests himself in the words and gestures of the assembly as it listens and responds to the proclamation of God's Word and as it gathers around the altar to give thanks and praise and receive the body and blood of Christ.[21] Among the symbols of the liturgy the assembly of believers is of particular importance.[22]

24. It is likewise Catholic belief that Christ is truly present in the Word, "since it is he himself who speaks when the holy Scriptures are read in the Church."[23] Thus the Church has always revered sacred Scripture even as it has revered the Body of the Lord, because, above all in the liturgy, it never ceases to receive the Bread of Life from the table both of God's Word and of Christ's Body and Blood.[24] The Second Vatican Council likened the Bible to a fountain of inner renewal within the community of God's people, and directed that in the revision of liturgical celebrations there should be more reading from Scripture.[25] Thus it is seen that by means of the Scriptures proclaimed and explained within the liturgy "God is speaking to his people, opening up to them the mystery of redemption and salvation, and nourishing their spirit; Christ is present to the faithful through his own word."[26]

25. The ordained ministers of the Church have the responsibility of presiding over the prayer which builds up the Church. Through the minister the voice of Christ himself calls, invokes, challenges, proclaims, and encourages. This manifestation of Christ, of course, is most clearly seen in the bishop or priest who presides at the eucharist. By virtue of priestly ordination, he acts in the person of Christ when he prays, presides over the assembly, and speaks on behalf of all present.[27]

26.   Through ordination the deacon also has the responsibility of leading the prayer of the assembly, since he "has been ordained for the nurture and increase of the people of God."[28] For this reason, all things being equal, the diocesan bishop should give preference to the appointment of deacons as presiding ministers at Sunday worship in the absence of a priest.

27.   Likewise a layperson who has been appointed by the bishop may be given the responsibility of leading worship in the absence of a priest or deacon. Although not ordained, a layperson leads the prayer of a community by virtue of that common priesthood which each Christian shares through baptism and confirmation.[29]

28.   Finally, and above all, Christ is uniquely present in the eucharistic elements under the appearances of bread and wine at each celebration of the eucharist. This presence continues even after the celebration has concluded. The Church accordingly reserves the consecrated elements for the communion of the sick and viaticum for the dying, and for the adoration of the faithful. The reservation of the sacrament of Christ's body and blood also makes it possible for communities without a priest to receive holy communion when Mass cannot be celebrated; this practice is to be encouraged. The eucharist is reserved under the form of the consecrated bread, except in those circumstances where the sick are able to receive communion only under the form of the consecrated wine (see *Pastoral Care of the Sick*, no. 74). The pastor should see that the eucharist is brought at least weekly to the community from the parish or other community where the eucharist has been celebrated. This will serve to strengthen the bonds between the community without a priest, its pastor, and the other communities where the eucharist is celebrated.

IV. THE LEADER AT A SUNDAY CELEBRATION IN THE ABSENCE OF A PRIEST

29.   When the Sunday Mass cannot be celebrated because there is no assigned priest or because the priest is legitimately unavailable, the diocesan bishop, in consultation with the pastor, may appoint a deacon or, if necessary, another person, lay or religious, to lead one of the several liturgical rites provided in *Sunday Celebrations in the Absence of a Priest: Leader's Edition*. If desired, the bishop may determine a specific term for this appointment, and its renewal may be subject to review.

30. Those so chosen for this ministry should be trained to lead each of these liturgical rites: Morning Prayer, Evening Prayer, and the Celebration of the Liturgy of the Word, all of which may include the distribution of holy communion. In addition, especially when these ministers also serve as the pastoral administrators of parishes, they should be well versed in the administration of communion to the sick and viaticum to the dying, in preaching (when specifically designated), in the exposition of the holy eucharist, in those rites from the *Order of Christian Funerals* which, on occasion, they may be required to lead, and in other liturgical and devotional services.

SELECTION

31. Each diocese should establish its own procedures for the selection of suitable candidates for formation in leading the Sunday assembly in worship. Pastoral insight must be exercised in the selection of those to be trained and commissioned to serve in such a capacity.

32. Those chosen for this ministry should not merely be "volunteers," but persons who exhibit a living appreciation for Scripture, a deep reverence for the eucharist, an active prayer life, an exemplary moral life, a spirit of cooperation with the laity and clergy of the particular community, an acceptance by the members of the community, an active involvement in the pastoral life of the community, and both a strong desire and ability to foster participation by lay people as members of the worshiping assembly and in other liturgical roles. The cultural make-up and linguistic needs of the assembly should also be considered in the selection of candidates.

33. Moreover, the candidates should demonstrate the necessary skills for public speaking which will enable them to be heard and understood in a liturgical setting, as well as the requisite sense of presence that is called for in movement and gesture in prayer. Finally, there should be evidence of the persons' commitment to this ministry, of their availability to exercise it, and of their willingness and ability to integrate within a solid spirituality the exercise of this ministry with personal and family obligations.

34. In parishes and missions where Sunday celebrations in the absence of a priest may be required on a regular basis, e.g., bi-weekly or monthly, it is recommended that a minimum of two candidates receive formation in exercising the ministry of leading Sunday celebrations.

TRAINING

35. Each candidate for the role of leader should complete the program of training and formation required by the diocese. This training will help the candidate to learn what the ministry requires with respect to knowledge of the Church's faith and tradition, as these are expressed in its worship life, and what the leadership of the local assembly in the expression of its faith requires. The training sessions should include a study of the sacramental and prayer life of the Church and its sources and spirituality, the theology of ministry, formation in the Scriptures and in the ministry of preaching, the *Liturgy of the Hours*, the rite of holy communion outside Mass, the liturgical year, devotions in the life of the Church, a familiarity with the *Lectionary for Mass*, the *Sacramentary*, and other liturgical books, and a practicum in liturgical presidency.

COMMISSIONING

36. Upon completion of the course of formation, the bishop or his delegate should commission the new ministers. The "Order for the Blessing of Those Who Exercise Pastoral Service," contained in the American edition of the *Book of Blessings*, might be used or adapted. (Deacons, by their ordination, are ordinary ministers of the eucharist and have received the commission to preside at Christian worship. However, it may on occasion be possible to include them in a service led by the bishop or his delegate which bestows a mandate for leadership in a specific community, while, at the same time, acknowledging that they are ordained ministers of the Church.) The initial designation to function in this ministry should be established for a specific place and period of time, after which, upon a favorable evaluation of an individual's service, the bishop's appointment may be renewed.

37. The commissioning rite may be celebrated in the parish church of the candidates. However, when candidates from several parishes are commissioned by the bishop at the cathedral church, it is appropriate that members of their communities be present at the commissioning along with the clergy, and the family and friends of the candidates. In such cases, it is recommended that a brief letter from the bishop be read to the community of the newly commissioned minister on the first Sunday that minister leads the community's Sunday worship.

CONTINUING FORMATION

38. Those who exercise the role of leading Sunday celebrations in the absence of a priest bear a responsibility for continued personal growth in the Lord through prayer and study beyond the formation period itself. If their ministry is not to become routine and perfunctory, they will need to root themselves ever more deeply in the mystery of life in Christ. Of special value will be retreats and days of recollection, parish adult education programs, and workshops sponsored by the diocese that address the needs of sacred worship. The reading of periodicals and books on liturgy and prayer, and the study of Scripture will also serve to nourish not only these ministers but also those they serve. Parishes would do well to make such periodicals available to all who exercise liturgical ministries on their behalf.

V. GENERAL PRINCIPLES OF LITURGICAL PRAYER THAT APPLY TO SUNDAY CELEBRATIONS IN THE ABSENCE OF A PRIEST

39. Several fundamental principles concerning liturgical prayer provide assistance in correctly understanding the nature of Sunday celebrations in the absence of a priest. These principles must be kept in mind when planning the celebrations.

PROCLAMATION OF THE PASCHAL MYSTERY

40. "Themes" are never arbitrarily to be imposed on the liturgy. Rather the assembly's Sunday worship always flows from four interrelated liturgical factors. Foremost among them is the understanding that at the center of all Christian worship is the proclamation of the paschal mystery: the Good News of God's marvelous plan whereby the scattered children of God have been gathered together in love through the life, death, and resurrection of Jesus Christ.

41. The second factor which shapes the liturgy on any given Lord's Day is the liturgical year. The Sundays and seasons of Advent, Christmas, Lent, Easter, and Ordinary Time and the other elements of liturgical time (sunrise and sunset, vigils and octaves, and particular festivals) provide the setting through which the community gains an understanding of the meaning and celebrates a particular facet of the mystery of God's love in Jesus Christ.

42. God's saving plan, unfolded in the course of the Church's year, is illumined further by the Scripture readings assigned in the *Lectionary for Mass*. Through the appointed Scripture readings of the *Lectionary*, the Church reaches a more specific statement of the Good News by which the members are spiritually nourished.

43. Finally, this proclamation of the paschal mystery must be related to the living, human experience of a specific group of people at a particular time and place. In light of this factor the leader and all who prepare the liturgy should mold the explanation of the Scriptures, the general intercessions, the choices made among prayer texts where options are provided, the selection of music, and the composition of introductions to the needs of the worshiping community.[30]

THE NECESSITY OF PREPARING
THE CELEBRATION

44. In order to ensure that the Sunday celebration be done as well as possible, care should be taken to prepare carefully all the elements of the celebration: the ministers, the liturgical texts, the actions and gestures, the music, the liturgical environment, and the assembly itself. This should be done in collaboration with the parish or community liturgical committee.

LITURGICAL TEXTS

45. The *Liturgy of the Hours*, the *Sacramentary*, the *Lectionary for Mass*, *Holy Communion and Worship of the Eucharist Outside Mass*, and the other approved ritual books offer a variety of prayers, readings, and other texts for Sunday celebrations in the absence of a priest. In order to assist ministers, the National Conference of Catholic Bishops has prepared *Sunday Celebrations in the Absence of a Priest: Leader's Edition*, a ritual book composed of texts taken from the above-mentioned sources. On Sundays and solemnities no substitutions should be made for the readings given in the *Lectionary* and the Prayer of the Day (used as the opening prayer or the concluding prayer) since these have been chosen with the whole Church in mind.[31] But whenever optional texts are provided, the leader and those who assist in preparing for the celebration should make use of the options allowed. These options might include the choice of particular readings and presidential prayers, etc. However, the basic structure of the rite itself should not be changed or adapted, even by the leader. "Liturgical services are not private functions but are celebrations of the Church."[32]

MINISTERS

46. In addition to the leader, a full complement of trained and prepared ministers should participate in each celebration: readers, musicians, cantors, choir, acolytes, ministers of hospitality (ushers), and any other ministers required for the celebration. "In liturgical celebrations each one, minister or layperson, who has an office to perform, should do all of, but only, those parts which pertain to that office by the nature of the rite and the principles of liturgy."[33] Hence, the leader should not assume the roles and function of other ministers.

MUSIC

47. The musical principles given in the introductions to the various rites of the Church, as well as those provided by the Committee on the Liturgy of the National Conference of Catholic Bishops, such as *Music in Catholic Worship* (1972; revised edition, 1983) and *Liturgical Music Today* (1982), are to be applied to Sunday celebrations in the absence of a priest. At a celebration of the Liturgy of the Hours, the principle of progressive solemnity should guide the choice of sung settings of the various elements.[34] Similarly, the musical requirements for celebrations of the Word and the distribution of holy communion are similar to those for the celebration of the eucharist, except for those elements of the Mass which are not included (i.e., the preparation of the altar and the gifts, the eucharistic prayer, and the breaking of the bread).

48. Since the liturgy is an action of the whole assembly, the first attention of leaders and music planners should be given to the moments of sung prayer which belong to the whole assembly, namely, the entrance song, the responsorial psalm, the gospel acclamation, and, when communion is distributed, the communion song. After that music has been planned, with special attention to seasonal and particular needs, other congregational, choral, vocal, or instrumental music may be chosen. In particular circumstances the use of music in more than one language may be appropriate. All musical choices, including the manner in which the music will be performed, must serve the shape and dynamics of the entire liturgy, as well as its basic structure.

SILENCE

49. Silence serves as a positive and necessary element within the structure of worship. It is important because it provides the community with the opportunity for personal reflection. A period of silence should be observed after the invitations to prayer, i.e., "Let us pray," the Scripture readings, and the communion song.[35]

THE ENVIRONMENT FOR WORSHIP

50. A carefully prepared environment will convey the message and spirit of celebration to the community as it enters the area for worship. Vesture, lighting, the effective use of colors, candles, incense, live plants, an attractive *Lectionary* and *Book of Gospels* (when available), incense and candles at the proclamation of the Gospel (when judged appropriate)—all have a great effect on the mood of the celebration. Attention should also be given to the cultural life, religious symbols, and artistic expressions of a particular community. Whenever possible, attempts should be made to integrate them into the liturgical environment.

MOVEMENT, GESTURE, AND POSTURE

51. The words and music of the community's prayer should be balanced and focused by attention given to movement, gesture, and posture. The care with which these bodily elements of worship are approached by those who prepare the liturgy, the leader, the other ministers, and the entire assembly will affect the prayer of all present.

VI. THE STRUCTURE OF SUNDAY CELEBRATIONS IN THE ABSENCE OF A PRIEST

52. Two options are provided for Sunday worship in the absence of a priest: the celebration of Morning or Evening Prayer from the Liturgy of the Hours, or the celebration of the Liturgy of the Word, all of which may include the distribution of holy communion.

MORNING OR EVENING PRAYER

53. Morning Prayer and Evening Prayer both have the same structure and the following elements:

Introductory Rites. These rites (Invitatory and Hymn) serve to gather the faithful into a worshiping community.

Psalmody. The singing or recitation of psalms and scriptural canticles, along with their respective antiphons and optional psalm-prayers, permits the assembly to join its praise and thanksgiving to God to that of Christ, who is our great high priest and advocate.

Liturgy of the Word. The proclamation of the Scripture readings assigned in the *Lectionary for Mass* brings to those gathered in faith the message of the good news of salvation and redemption in Christ. The response of the assembly to the Word of God is a combination of thanksgiving (Canticle of Zechariah or Canticle of Mary) for God's goodness to us, and of intercession (Intercessions) for the needs of the Church and the world.

Communion Rite. The assembly unites itself to the paschal mystery of Christ in holy communion. The reception of communion is also a sign and expression of the assembly's union with those who are able to celebrate the eucharist on that particular day. If holy communion is not distributed, this portion of the rite is omitted.

Concluding Rite. After having heard the Word of God (and having been nourished by the body and blood of Christ in holy communion), the assembly is sent forth with God's blessing to live the Christian life.

LITURGY OF THE WORD

54. When the Sunday celebration takes the form of a celebration of the Liturgy of the Word, it includes the following elements:

Introductory Rites. The purpose of these rites is to form the gathered faithful into a community and to dispose them for the celebration.

Liturgy of the Word. God speaks to his people through the Scripture readings assigned in the *Lectionary for Mass*, disclosing to them the mystery of redemption and salvation; the people respond through the profession of faith and the general intercessions.

Thanksgiving. The community blesses God for the gift of redemption in Christ.

Communion Rite. This rite is an expression and accomplishment of communion with Christ and with his members, especially with those who on this same day take part in the eucharistic sacrifice. If holy communion is not distributed, this portion of the rite is omitted.

Concluding Rites. The blessing and dismissal point to the connection existing between the liturgy and the Christian life.

SPECIFIC NORMS

55. In either form of the Sunday celebration the following particular points should be kept in mind by those responsible for planning the celebration and by the leader.

    A.   The person who leads the community at a Sunday celebration in the absence of a priest, whether a deacon or layperson, is called the "leader."

    B.   The leader may be vested in lay clothing or religious habit, a well-designed alb, or other suitable vesture according to diocesan policy. The use of the stole and dalmatic is reserved to deacons.

    C.   Laypersons are to avoid all things proper to a priest or deacon. They do not use the greeting before the Gospel ("The Lord be with you") or any of the other greetings designated for a deacon or priest. Nor do they use the priestly or diaconal forms of blessing. *Sunday Celebrations in the Absence of a Priest:*

Leader's Edition provides proper forms of blessing for laypersons. When giving a blessing, a layperson does not make the sign of the cross over the people.

D. The chair used by a layperson must be different from the presidential chair used by a priest or deacon, and normally it should be placed outside the presbyterium in close proximity to the assembly. The ambo is reserved for the Liturgy of the Word. The altar is used only when the eucharist is placed on it before the distribution of holy communion, if it is included in the celebration.

E. The readings assigned in the *Lectionary* for a particular Sunday, solemnity, or feast are always to be used. On occasions when there are no assigned readings or when a selection is provided, the minister may choose appropriate readings. On Sundays and solemnities three readings are used, as at Mass. Whenever possible a sung responsorial psalm should follow the first reading.

F. The preaching of a homily is part of most liturgical rites and is, by its very definition, reserved to a priest or deacon.[36] However, the bishop may allow a layperson who is properly trained to explain the Word of God at Sunday celebrations in the absence of a priest or deacon and at other specified occasions.[37]

The pastor may provide a text for the leader to read,[38] or if the bishop has authorized the leader to preach, the minister preaches in his/her own words. It is essential that when the leader is to preach, the text should be prepared well in advance.

Preaching, an irreplaceable ministry for explaining the Scriptures and applying them to the here-and-now of a particular gathering, is a task to be taken seriously by those who have been duly delegated by the bishop. When one preaches in the name of the Church, the great public work of Christ is continued. For deacons, and for those laypersons who may be delegated to preach within the Lord's Day assembly, a diligence in prayer, commitment to the study of Scripture, growth in faith, and preparation are required.[39]

G. Candles may be used in the entrance procession or placed near the ambo. When the distribution of holy communion concludes the celebration, candles are lighted at the altar before the sacrament is brought to it from the place of reservation.

H. A layperson, delegated by the bishop, may impart any of the blessings given in the *Book of Blessings* which are not reserved to a bishop, priest, or deacon.

VII. CATECHESIS

56.　It is essential that before Sunday celebrations in the absence of a priest are begun in a particular community there be a period of thorough catechesis on the importance of Sunday worship, the reasons for having these celebrations, and the need for prayer and other means of encouragement for more vocations to the priesthood. It is especially important that the community be assisted in deepening its understanding of the importance of the sacramental worship of the Church and its ordained ministry, lest, in time, Sunday worship in the absence of a priest come to be seen as normative.

57.　Catechesis directed to the Sunday assembly should clearly state the Church's teaching on the meaning of the Mass as found in the *General Instruction of the Roman Missal.*[40] The catechesis should explain the very nature of the eucharist and the difference between the distribution of holy communion outside Mass and the celebration of Mass. Because of this difference, only a bishop or priest may preside at the eucharist, while a deacon, acolyte, or other specially designated minister may distribute holy communion.[41] Although a celebration of the Liturgy of the Word followed by the rite for the distribution of holy communion outside Mass parallels in a general fashion the structure of the Mass—introductory rites, celebration of the Word of God, reception of holy communion, and concluding rite—the essential element of the full eucharistic action, the eucharistic prayer and the usual rites for preparing the altar and the gifts of bread and wine, are not included. Reception of communion at such a liturgical celebration is from the reserved sacrament consecrated at an earlier celebration of Mass, particularly a Mass celebrated the same day (or preceding evening). Thus, in referring to these Sunday celebrations, the expression that a layperson or a deacon is "celebrating Mass" is to be studiously avoided.

58.　When due to necessity Christians receive communion outside of Mass, "they are closely united with the sacrifice which perpetuates the sacrifice of the cross."[42] The sacred species themselves are reserved in Catholic churches for sharing communion, especially with the sick, and viaticum with the dying, and for that worship of the eucharist which flows from the Mass. It is always the celebration of the eucharist itself which is at once the origin and the goal of the reverence which is shown the eucharist outside the Mass.[43]

CONCLUSION

59.　The preparation of this statement and *Sunday Celebrations in the Absence of a Priest: Leader's Edition* has been a major project for the Bishops' Committee on the Liturgy. The committee wishes to thank all those who assisted in this work and is especially appreciative of all the bishops who cooperated in the survey it conducted in 1987.

60. The task group that was established by the Liturgy Committee to prepare these documents quickly learned of the complexity of the problem on both the theological and pastoral levels. It also discovered that proposed solutions did not really deal with the root problem. The primary need for having Sunday celebrations in the absence of a priest is the lack of a sufficient number of priests or, at least, an inequitable distribution of priests so that some regions of the country have large numbers of priests and others are forced to place several parishes under a single pastor. Until a solution is found for the lack of a sufficient number of priests, the need for Sunday celebrations in the absence of a priest will continue and, according to the survey conducted by the Bishops' Committee on the Liturgy in 1987, the need will increase at least through the next several years.

61. On the positive side, it is clear that Sunday celebrations under the leadership of a deacon or layperson will enable a community to continue to worship and be nourished by the Word of God and the eucharist. Such celebrations allow Catholics to take responsibility for prayer and worship in the absence of their own priest, a responsibility that flows from their baptism and confirmation.

62. However, at best these celebrations are only a temporary measure. The community is deprived of the celebration of the eucharist, and holy communion is separated from the Mass. There is a danger of a return to the situation of the past in which the Mass was seen only as a means for providing consecrated hosts for communion. The positive effects of the liturgical reform and renewal which have affirmed the Mass as the fount and summit of the Church's life are endangered by the practical need for these celebrations. Another danger which may arise is the acceptance of the notion of the Church as a local community with little or no direct connection to the diocese and the universal Church. It can easily lead to a sense of self-sufficiency that sees little or no need for ordained ministers. The challenge that faces the Church is to ensure that parishes and other communities that do not have a priest remain closely connected to the life of the diocese, and that Mass be celebrated in them as frequently as possible.

63. The Bishops' Committee on the Liturgy is convinced that in the present circumstances providing Sunday celebrations under the leadership of a deacon or designated layperson is the best response to the phenomenon of the "priestless Sunday." These celebrations enable communities gathered in steadfast faith to hear and respond to God's

Word, to be strengthened and nourished by the body and blood of Christ, and to continue to do the work of Christ in the world. However, it remains for the entire Church to continue to work and pray for more laborers for the harvest, more shepherds for the sheep. The Church has faced similar problems in the past and with a faith-filled hope now looks to the future and to the continuing renewal of all the People of God.

NOTES

1. See Vatican Council II, *Constitution on the Liturgy* (*Sacrosanctum Concilium*) [hereafter SC] (4 December 1963), art. 10; the English translation is from *Documents on the Liturgy 1965-1979: Conciliar, Papal, and Curial Texts* [hereafter DOL] (Collegeville, Minn.: The Liturgical Press, 1982), 1, no. 10.

2. Congregation for Divine Worship, circular letter *Eucharistiae participationem* (27 April 1973), no. 11 [DOL 248, no. 1985].

3. Justin Martyr (ca. 150 A.D.), 1 *Apology* 67:3-7, English translation by Edward Rochie Hardy, from *Early Christian Fathers*, Cyril C. Richardson, ed. (New York: Macmillan Publishing Co. Inc., 1970), 287.

4. *Bibliographica hagiographica latina*, no. 7492, in Peter G. Cobb, "The History of the Christian Year" in *The Study of Liturgy*, Cheslyn Jones, Geoffrey Wainwright, and Edward Yarnold, eds. (New York: Oxford University Press, 1978), 405.

5. *Didascalia* 21; see Cobb, 405.

6. Tertullian, *On the Crown* 3; see Cobb, 405.

7. Tertullian, *On Prayer* 23; Canon 20 of the Council of Nicaea; see Cobb, 405.

8. These effects flowing from the Sunday celebration have not always been adequately perceived or appreciated by Catholic Christians. In the Middle Ages the Church found it necessary to impose a law which commanded the observance of Sunday through participation in the Mass and by abstinence from all unnecessary work. Such a law remains to this day (see 1983 *Code of Canon Law* [hereafter CIC], canon 1247. It should be noted, however, that canon 1248 recognizes that at times participation in the eucharist is impossible either because no priest is available or for some other grave cause. In such cases, "it is specially recommended that the faithful take part in the liturgy of the word if it is celebrated in the parish church or in another sacred place according to the prescriptions of the diocesan bishop, or engage in prayer for an appropriate amount of time personally or in a family or, as occasion offers, in groups of families.") Thus the faithful have the duty of regularly taking part in Sunday worship not merely because of a legal precept, but as an expression of the virtue of religion, of gratitude and love for God, and in witness to those who do not know the Lord. In their catechesis on Sunday celebrations in the absence of a priest, diocesan bishops should ensure proper instruction on the precept of participating in Mass on Sundays and holy days of obligation and the obligations of those who are unable to do so because of the lack of a priest or some other grave circumstance.

9. Joint Synod of the Dioceses of the Federal Republic of Germany, Resolution on the Liturgy (21 November 1975), no. 2.1. Typescript copy.

10. Sacred Congregation of Rites, Instruction *Eucharisticum mysterium* [hereafter EM] (25 May 1967), no. 25 [DOL 179, no. 1254].

11. Congregation for Divine Worship, *General Instruction of the Roman Missal* [hereafter GIRM], 4th ed. (27 March 1975), no. 1 [DOL 208, no. 1391].

12. Leo the Great, "Sermon 63," in EM, no. 7 [DOL 179, no. 1236], see also Vatican Council II, *Dogmatic Constitution on the Church (Lumen gentium)* (21 November 1964), art. 26 [DOL 4, no. 146].

13. In *Epist. 1 ad Cor. Hom. 27*, in Cobb, 405.

14. Although, in certain circumstances, it may be the pastoral decision of the diocesan bishop to close a parish or combine one or more parishes or communities into a new parish or community with a common church or other place for the Sunday celebration of the eucharist, this document is concerned with circumstances where parishes or communities continue, but without the regular weekly celebration of Mass on Sunday.

15. See Congregation for Divine Worship, *Directory for Sunday Celebrations in the Absence of a Priest* [hereafter *Directory*], (2 June 1988), no. 18.

16. See CIC, can. 1248, par. 2.

17. Canadian Conference of Catholic Bishops, "Sunday Liturgy: When Lay People Preside," *National Bulletin on Liturgy* 14 (May/June 1981), 102-103.

18. Congregation for Divine Worship, *Holy Communion and Worship of the Eucharist Outside Mass* [hereafter HCWEOM] (21 June 1973), General Introduction, no. 6 [DOL 279, no. 2198]. The internal reference in this quotation is from the encyclical of Paul VI, *Mysterium fidei* (3 September 1965), no. 39 [DOL 176, no. 1183].

19. Ephesians 2:15-23; 3:9-10; 3:19; 5:18.

20. Matthew 18:20; 1 Corinthians 5:4.

21. See Bishops' Committee on the Liturgy, National Conference of Catholic Bishops, *Environment and Art in Catholic Worship*, 1978, no. 29.

22. Ibid., no. 28.

23. SC, art. 7 [DOL 1, no. 7].

24. See Vatican Council II, *Dogmatic Constitution on Divine Revelation (Dei verbum)* (18 November 1965), art. 21 [DOL 24, no. 224].

25. SC, art. 35 [DOL 1, no. 35].

26. GIRM, no. 33 [DOL 208, no. 1423].

27. SC, art. 33 [DOL 1, no. 33].

28. *Directory*, no. 29.

29. *Directory*, no. 30.

30. SC, art. 35.3 [DOL 1, no. 35]. GIRM, nos. 11 and 13 [DOL 208, nos. 1401 and 1403].

31. See GIRM, nos. 11 and 332 [DOL 208, no. 1401 and 1722].

32. SC, art. 26 [DOL 1, no. 26].

33. Ibid., art. 28 [DOL 1, no. 28].

34. *General Instruction of the Liturgy of the Hours*, nos. 273-277 [DOL 426, nos. 3703-3707].

35. SC, art. 30 [DOL 1, no. 30]. GIRM, nos. 23, 56, and 121 [DOL 208, nos. 1413, 1446, and 1511].

36. CIC, can. 767, §1.

37. Ibid., can. 766.

38. In some circumstances it may be desirable for the pastor to send a recorded message or homily to the community.

39. See the statement of the Bishops' Committee on Priestly Life and Ministry, *Fulfilled in Your Hearing* (Washington, D.C.: USCC, 1982), which offers a brief yet thorough introduction to the task and method of preaching.

40. GIRM, Introduction and chapter 1 [DOL 208, nos. 1376- 1396].

41. HCWEOM, no. 17 [DOL 266, no. 2095].

42. HCWEOM, no. 15 [DOL 266, no. 2093].

43. EM, no. 3 [DOL 179, no. 1232].

SUNDAY CELEBRATIONS IN THE ABSENCE OF A PRIEST: LEADER'S EDITION

DECREE OF THE
NATIONAL CONFERENCE OF
CATHOLIC BISHOPS

In accordance with the provisions of no. 41 of the *Directory for Sunday Celebrations in the Absence of a Priest*, promulgated by the Congregation for Divine Worship on 2 June 1988, *Sunday Celebrations in the Absence of a Priest: Leader's Edition* was approved for use by the members of the National Conference of Catholic Bishops in plenary assembly on 7 November 1989.

On 1 January 1994 *Sunday Celebrations in the Absence of a Priest: Leader's Edition* may be published and used in those dioceses where the diocesan bishop has given authorization for Sunday celebrations in the absence of a priest.

Given at the General Secretariat of the National Conference of Catholic Bishops, Washington, D.C., on 14 September 1993, the feast of the Holy Cross.

+ William H. Keeler
Archbishop of Baltimore
President
National Conference of Catholic Bishops

Robert N. Lynch
General Secretary

FOREWORD

In light of the need expressed by many conferences of bishops for the provision of liturgical celebrations for those places where a priest is not available to celebrate the eucharist each Sunday, the Congregation for Divine Worship has published a *Directory for Sunday Celebrations in the Absence of a Priest* (2 June 1988).[1] This Directory recalls the Church's teaching on the meaning of Sunday, indicates the conditions when such celebrations may legitimately take place, and provides guidelines for carrying out such celebrations correctly.

Since it is the responsibility of the conferences of bishops, as circumstances suggest, to determine these norms in greater detail and to adapt them to the culture and conditions of their people, the National Conference of Catholic Bishops has prepared *Sunday Celebrations in the Absence of a Priest: Leader's Edition* for use by deacons and laypersons who will lead such celebrations.[2]

In the process of preparing this ritual book, the Bishops' Committee on the Liturgy surveyed the dioceses of the United States in order to determine the need for Sunday celebrations in the absence of a priest and the frequency of such celebrations at the present time. On the basis of that study, the committee discovered that such services are a present pastoral necessity in many dioceses and may become even more necessary in the coming years.

Before Sunday celebrations in the absence of a priest are begun in any diocese or parish, it is essential that there be diocesan-wide catechesis on the nature of these celebrations and the necessity of fostering vocations to the priesthood so that eventually no community will be denied the Sunday celebration of the eucharist each week.

+Most Reverend Donald W. Trautman
Bishop of Erie
Chairman, Bishops' Committee on the Liturgy

SUNDAY AND
ITS OBSERVANCE

1. "By a tradition handed down from the apostles and having its origin from the very day of Christ's resurrection, the Church celebrates the paschal mystery every eighth day, which, with good reason, bears the name of the Lord's Day or Sunday."[1]

2. The New Testament and the Fathers of the Church give ample evidence that for the early Church Sunday was the "Lord's Day." For it was on Sunday that the Lord conquered sin and death and rose to new life. In our own time, the Second Vatican Council has reminded us: "On this day Christ's faithful must gather together, so that, by hearing the word of God and taking part in the eucharist, they may call to mind the passion, resurrection, and glorification of the Lord Jesus and may thank God, who 'has begotten them again unto a living hope through the resurrection of Jesus Christ from the dead'" (1 Peter 1:3).[2]

3. The complete liturgical celebration of Sunday is characterized by the gathering of the faithful to manifest the Church, not simply on their own initiative but as called together by God, that is, as the people of God in their organic structure, presided over by a priest, who acts in the person of Christ. Through the celebration of the liturgy of the Word the assembled faithful are instructed in the paschal mystery by the Scriptures which are proclaimed and which are then explained in the homily by a priest or deacon. And through the celebration of the liturgy of the eucharist, by which the paschal mystery is sacramentally effected, the assembly participates in the very sacrifice of Christ.[3]

4. Pastoral catechesis on the importance of Sunday should emphasize that the sacrifice of the Mass is the only true actualization of the Lord's paschal mystery[4] and is the most complete manifestation of the Church: "Hence the Lord's Day is the first holyday of all and should be proposed to the devotion of the faithful and taught to them. . . . Other celebrations, unless they be truly of greatest importance, shall not have precedence over the Sunday, the foundation and core of the whole liturgical year."[5]

5. In the Sunday assembly, as also in the life of the Christian community, the faithful should find both active participation and a true spirit of community, as well as the opportunity to be renewed spiritually under the guidance of the Holy Spirit.[6]

SUNDAY CELEBRATIONS IN THE ABSENCE OF A PRIEST

6. There have been and still are many of the faithful in the United States for whom, because of the lack of a priest or some other serious reason, participation in the eucharistic celebration demands a great sacrifice.[7]

7. In addition, because of the shortage of priests in certain areas, priests must celebrate Mass several times on Sundays in many widely scattered churches.[8] They are to be commended for their dedication and pastoral zeal.

8. In circumstances in which there is no reasonable opportunity to provide for the celebration of Mass, local bishops may judge it necessary to provide for other Sunday celebrations in the absence of a priest, so that in the best way possible the weekly gathering of the faithful can be continued and the Christian tradition regarding Sunday preserved.[9]

9. When on a particular Sunday even this kind of celebration is not possible, the faithful are strongly urged to devote themselves to prayer "for a suitable time either individually or with the family or, if possible, with a group of families."[10]

CONDITIONS FOR HOLDING SUNDAY CELEBRATIONS IN THE ABSENCE OF A PRIEST

10. When a priest cannot be present for the celebration of Mass on the Lord's Day, it is of paramount importance that the parish or mission community still come together to celebrate the resurrection of the Lord. If, in the judgment of the diocesan bishop, it is not practical or possible for the community to participate in the celebration of Mass in a church nearby,[11] they should assemble for Sunday worship in their own community under the leadership of the person the bishop and pastor have designated to lead them in prayer. In such a case the celebration takes one of the forms found in this ritual.

11. Before Sunday celebrations in the absence of a priest are begun, it should be explained to the faithful that although these celebrations substitute for the Sunday celebration of the eucharist, they should not be regarded as the ideal solution to present circumstances nor as a surrender to mere convenience.[12] There should normally be only one assembly of this kind in each place on any given Sunday.[13]

12. Any confusion in the minds of the faithful between this kind of assembly and a eucharistic celebration must be carefully avoided. These celebrations should increase the desire of the faithful to be present at and participate in the celebration of the eucharist.[14]

13. To this end, the faithful need to understand that the eucharistic sacrifice cannot take place without a priest and that the eucharistic communion which they may receive in this kind of assembly is closely connected with the sacrifice of the Mass.[15]

OFFICES AND MINISTRIES

BISHOP

14. It is the responsibility of the diocesan bishop, after having received the advice of the diocesan presbyteral council and, if appropriate, other consultative bodies, to decide whether Sunday celebrations in the absence of a priest should be held on an occasional or regular basis in his diocese. He is to set out general and particular norms for such celebrations. They are to be held only when and where approved by the bishop and only under the pastoral ministry of a priest who has the responsibility for the particular community.[16]

15. Before the bishop decides on having such Sunday celebrations, he should consider the possibility of recourse to priests, even religious priests, who are not directly assigned to the care of souls. At the same time, he should consider the frequency of Masses in the various parishes and churches of the diocese with a view toward freeing a priest to celebrate Mass with a community without its own priest.[17] The preeminence of the celebration of the eucharist, particularly on Sunday, over other pastoral activities is to be respected.[18]

16. The bishop should appoint a delegate or a special committee to ensure that the ministers who will lead the assembly are properly instructed and that these celebrations are carried out correctly. He is also to see to it that the people of the parish or community receive the necessary instruction. But the bishop's concern should always be that the faithful involved have the opportunity to participate in the celebration of the eucharist as often as possible, and at least several times a year.[19]

PASTOR

17. The pastor has the responsibility of informing the bishop about the need for such celebrations in the area under his pastoral care, to prepare the faithful for them, to visit them during the week, and at a convenient time to celebrate the sacraments with them, particularly the sacrament of penance. In this way the communities involved will come to realize that their assembly on Sunday is not an assembly "without a priest," but an assembly "in the absence of a priest," or, better still, an assembly "in expectation of a priest."[20]

DEACON

18. As a minister of the Word, who also has a responsibility for the sacraments, the deacon is called in a special way to lead these Sunday assemblies. Since the deacon has been ordained for the nurture and increase of the people of God, it belongs to him to lead the prayers, to proclaim the gospel, to preach the homily, and to give communion.[21]

19. When a deacon presides at a Sunday celebration in the absence of a priest, he acts in the usual manner in regard to the greetings, the prayers, the gospel reading and homily, the giving of communion, and the dismissal and blessing. He wears the vestments proper to his ministry, that is, the alb with stole, and, as circumstances suggest, the dalmatic. He uses the presidential chair.[22]

20. The deacon is always to be assisted by other ministers who will proclaim the Scriptures, assist him in the distribution of holy communion, sing the psalms and other songs, provide instrumental music, and prepare the place for the celebration.[23]

LAYPERSON

21. In the absence of both a priest and a deacon, upon the request and recommendation of the pastor, the bishop is to appoint persons, lay or religious, who are to be entrusted with the care of leading these celebrations, namely, with leading the prayers, with the ministry of the word, and, when it is to be included in the celebration, with giving holy communion.

These ministers carry out their responsibilities in virtue of their baptism and confirmation.[24] Such persons are to be chosen in view of the consistency of their way of life with the Gospel and in the expectation of their being acceptable to the community of the faithful. The appointment of such ministers is made by the bishop for a definite time. Their appointment is to be made known to the community by means of a liturgical celebration in which prayers are offered to God on behalf of those appointed. The Order for the Blessing of Those Who Exercise Pastoral Service[25] contained in the *Book of Blessings* may be used for this purpose.

The pastor is to see to the suitable and continuous instruction of these laypersons and to assist them in the preparation of worthy celebrations.[26]

22. The laypersons appointed as leaders should regard the office entrusted to them not so much as an honor but as a responsibility and, above all, as a service to their brothers and sisters under the authority of the pastor.[27] They "should do all of, but only, those parts which pertain to that office."[28] They should carry out their office with sincere devotion and the decorum demanded by such a responsibility and rightly expected of them by God's people.[29]

23. The leader who is a layperson uses the special forms indicated in the rites for the greeting and blessing, does not use words that are proper to a priest or deacon, and omits those rites, gestures, and texts that are too readily associated with the Mass and which might give the impression that the layperson is a sacred minister.[30]

24. The layperson wears vesture that is suitable for his or her function or the vesture prescribed by the bishop.[31] A layperson does not use the presidential chair.[32] Since the altar is the table of sacrifice and of the paschal banquet, its only use in one of these celebrations is for the rite of communion, when the eucharist is placed on it at the beginning of the communion rite.

The leader is always to be assisted by other ministers who will proclaim the Scriptures, assist in the distribution of holy communion, sing the psalms and other songs, provide instrumental music, and prepare the place for the celebration.[33]

FORMS THE SUNDAY CELEBRATION MAY TAKE

25. A common feature of the liturgical rites provided for the Sunday celebration in the absence of a priest is the proclamation of the Word of God. The aim of this provision is that the riches of Sacred Scripture and of the Church's prayer be amply provided to the faithful gathered on Sundays in various ways even apart from Mass. For the faithful should not be deprived of the readings that are read at Mass in the course of a year, nor of the prayers of the liturgical seasons.[34]

26. A second provision of the services which follow is the distribution of holy communion. Although the faithful cannot share in the actual celebration of the Mass, they nevertheless may be fed at the table of the Lord and be spiritually united to the community from which the holy eucharist was brought to the Sunday celebration.

According to circumstances, it may not always be possible to have the distribution of holy communion during the Sunday celebration. When this is the case, those present should be made to realize that, nevertheless, Christ is truly present in the gathered assembly and in the Scriptures that are proclaimed.[35]

LITURGY OF THE HOURS

27. The first form given for the Sunday celebration in the absence of a priest is that of Morning or Evening Prayer from *The Liturgy of the Hours*.[36] For "when the people are invited to the Liturgy of the Hours and come together in unity of heart and voice, they show forth the Church in its celebration of the mystery of Christ."[37] Holy communion may be given at the end of either Morning or Evening Prayer.[38]

28. Those responsible for the preparation and celebration of Morning or Evening Prayer should be familiar with the *General Instruction of the Liturgy of the Hours*[39] as well as the structure and contents of *The Liturgy of the Hours*.[40]

29. The texts provided for Morning Prayer (nos. 52-86) and Evening Prayer (nos. 87-121) are given as a common form and by way of example. The texts proper to each Sunday contained in *The Liturgy of the Hours* may always be used. In particular circumstances, it may be necessary to adapt the rite. When this is done, the order of the celebration and the essential elements, as given in the outlines before Morning and Evening Prayer, are to be maintained.

30. Music is an essential part of the divine office and should always be a part of each celebration. The amount of singing and the type of music used will depend on the musical resources that are available and the abilities of the members of the assembly to sing.

31. Morning and Evening Prayer both have the same structure and the following elements:

> *Introductory Rites*—These rites (Introduction and Hymn) serve to gather the faithful into a worshiping community.
>
> *Psalmody*—The singing or recitation of psalms and scriptural canticles, along with their respective antiphons and psalm-prayers, permits the assembly to join its praise and thanksgiving to God to that of Christ, who is our great high priest and advocate.
>
> *Liturgy of the Word*—The proclamation of the Scriptures to those gathered in faith brings them the message of the good news of salvation and redemption in Christ. The response of the assembly

to the Word of God is a combination of thanksgiving (Canticle of Zechariah or Canticle of Mary) for God's goodness to us, and of intercession (Intercessions) for the needs of the Church and the world.

[*Communion Rite*—The assembly unites itself to the paschal mystery of Christ in holy communion. It is also a sign and expression of the assembly's union with those who are able to celebrate the eucharist on that particular day.]

Concluding Rite—After having heard the Word of God (and having been nourished by the body and blood of Christ in holy communion), the assembly is sent forth with God's blessing to live the Christian life.

LITURGY OF THE WORD

32. Among the forms of celebration found in liturgical tradition when Mass is not possible, a celebration of the Word of God is particularly recommended.[41] This celebration may be concluded by eucharistic communion, when possible. In this way the faithful can be nourished by both the Word of God and the body of Christ. "By hearing the Word of God the faithful learn that the marvels it proclaims reach their climax in the paschal mystery, of which the Mass is a sacramental memorial and in which they share by communion."[42] Further, in certain circumstances the Sunday celebration may be combined with the celebration of baptism, marriage, or blessings in ways that are suited to the needs of each community.[43]

33. The order to be followed in this form of the Sunday celebration consists of the celebration of the Word of God and may also include the giving of holy communion. Nothing that is proper to Mass, and particularly the presentation of the gifts and the eucharistic prayer, is to be inserted into the celebration.[44]

34. The texts of the prayers and readings for each Sunday, solemnity, or feast of the Lord are taken from *The Roman Missal* (*Sacramentary*) and the *Lectionary for Mass*. This allows the faithful to follow the cycle of the liturgical year and pray and listen to the Word of God in communion with the other communities of the Church.[45] The prayers from the *Sacramentary* are contained in Appendix III of this ritual [available in the complete version of *The Leader's Edition*].

35. Those who are responsible for the preparation and celebration of this form of the Sunday celebration should be familiar with the principles found in the *General Instruction of the Roman Missal*[46] and the Introduction of the *Lectionary for Mass*.[47]

36. The following is an outline of the elements of the celebration:

Introductory Rites—The purpose of these rites is to form the gathered faithful into a community and for them to dispose themselves for the celebration.

Liturgy of the Word—God speaks to his people, to disclose to them the mystery of redemption and salvation; the people respond through the profession of faith and the general intercessions.

Thanksgiving–God is blessed for his great glory.

[*Communion Rite*—This rite is an expression and accomplishment of communion with Christ and with his members, especially with those who on this same day take part in the eucharistic sacrifice.]

Concluding Rites—The blessing and dismissal point to the connection existing between the liturgy and the Christian life.[48]

INDIVIDUAL PARTS OF ALL SUNDAY CELEBRATIONS

INTRODUCTORY RITES

37. In the introduction at the beginning of the celebration, or at some other point, the leader should inform the assembly where the pastor is celebrating the eucharist on that particular Sunday and urge the assembly to unite itself in spirit with that community.[49]

PSALMODY

38. The singing of psalms is included in every Sunday celebration. Psalmody lies at the core of Morning and Evening Prayer. By the use of the psalms the Church unites the praise of the Church on earth to that of the saints. The responsorial psalm in the liturgy of the Word allows the assembly to respond to the Word of God and reflect upon it.

LITURGY OF THE WORD

39. Normally there are three readings as at the Sunday Mass. The first reading is followed by a responsorial psalm and the second reading is followed by the gospel acclamation.

40. The first two readings are proclaimed by one or two readers. The Gospel is proclaimed by the leader. A layperson omits the greeting, "The Lord be with you," before the Gospel.

41. In order that the assembly may retain the Word of God, there should be an explanation of the readings or a period of silence for reflection on what has been heard. Since only an ordained minister may give a homily,[50] the pastor may prepare a homily for the leader to read.[51] In other cases when a layperson has been permitted to preach by the bishop, he or she may give those present a brief explanation of the biblical text, so that they may understand through faith the meaning of the celebration.

42. The general intercessions follow the established series of intentions as is indicated in Appendix I.[52] Particular intentions for the whole diocese proposed by the bishop are always to be included. Intentions for vocations to sacred orders, for the bishop, and for the pastor should often be included in the general intercessions.[53]

ACT OF THANKSGIVING

43. At the celebration of Morning and Evening Prayer from *The Liturgy of the Hours,* thanksgiving is expressed by the psalms and canticles. When holy communion is distributed at the end of either Morning or Evening Prayer, a psalm, hymn, or litany of praise and thanksgiving may follow communion.

44. At a celebration of a liturgy of the Word, the act of thanksgiving is part of the communal response to the Word of God, and when communion is distributed it is an expression of gratitude for being able to participate in this sacrament.

While no. 45 of the *Directory* provides several positions for the thanksgiving, the National Conference of Catholic Bishops has determined that it should take place in the following manner.

After the general intercessions, the leader invites all to an act of thanksgiving, in which the faithful praise the glory and mercy of God. This can be done by use of a psalm (for example, Psalms 100, 113, 118, 136, 147, 150), a hymn (for example, the *Gloria*), a canticle (for example, the Canticle of Mary), a litany, or a prayer. The leader and the faithful stand and, facing the altar, together recite the thanksgiving. Additional texts for the act of thanksgiving are given in Appendix II.

In order to avoid all confusion between the eucharistic prayer of the Mass and the prayer of thanksgiving used in these Sunday celebrations, these prayers of thanksgiving are not to take the form of a eucharistic prayer or preface.[54]

COMMUNION RITE

45. When holy communion is to be given, the provisions given in *The Roman Ritual* for communion outside Mass are to be observed.[55] The faithful are to be frequently reminded that even when they receive communion outside Mass they are united to the eucharistic sacrifice.[56]

46. When Mass cannot be celebrated, the pastor will see to it that frequent opportunities are provided for giving holy communion. He is also to see to it that there is a celebration of the eucharist in due time in each community. The consecrated hosts are to be renewed often and kept in a safe place.[57]

47. For communion, if at all possible, eucharistic Bread consecrated that same Sunday in a Mass celebrated elsewhere is used; a deacon or layperson brings it in a ciborium or another vessel and places it in the tabernacle before the celebration. Eucharistic Bread consecrated at the last Mass celebrated in the place of assembly may also be used. Before the Lord's Prayer the leader goes to the tabernacle or place where the eucharist is reserved, takes the vessel with the body of the Lord, and places it upon the table of the altar.[58] A leader who is a layperson then returns to his or her chair and introduces the Lord's Prayer. After the sign of peace the leader goes to the altar for the invitation to communion.[59] A deacon remains at the altar for the Lord's Prayer and the sign of peace.

48. The Lord's Prayer is always recited or sung by all, even if there is to be no communion. The sign of peace may be exchanged. After communion, "a period of silence may be observed or a psalm or song of praise may be sung."[60]

CONCLUDING RITE

49. Before the conclusion of the assembly, announcements or notices relating to the life of the parish or the diocese are read.[61] The collection of monetary gifts of the assembly may also be done at this time.

PREPARATIONS FOR THE SUNDAY CELEBRATION

50. The leader or some other person should see to the preparation of the church or place where the celebration will take place. The following preparations are made:

The *Lectionary for Mass* is prepared before the celebration. It may be carried in the entrance procession, if there is one, or placed on the lectern.

When Morning or Evening Prayer or a liturgy of the Word is celebrated without the distribution of holy communion, lighted candles may be placed near the ambo.

The decorations of the church or place of celebration should be in accord with the liturgical season being celebrated.

When communion is given in a church or oratory, a corporal is to be placed on the altar, which is already covered with a cloth. When communion is given in other places, a suitable table is to be prepared and covered with a cloth. Lighted candles are placed on or near the altar or table.[62]

51. In preparing the celebration the pastor, together with the appointed deacons and/or laypersons, may make adaptations suited to the number of those who will take part in the celebration, the ability of the leader of the assembly and other ministers, and the kind of instruments available for the music and the singing.[63]

NOTES

FOREWORD

1. Congregation for Divine Worship, *Directory for Sunday Celebration in the Absence of a Priest* (hereafter *Directory*), (2 June 1988).
2. See *Directory*, no. 7.

SUNDAY CELEBRATIONS IN THE ABSENCE OF A PRIEST: LEADER'S EDITION

1. Vatican Council II, Constitution on the Liturgy *Sacrosanctum Concilium* (hereafter, SC), art. 106: taken from *Documents on the Liturgy, 1963-1979: Conciliar, Papal, and Curial Texts*, International Commission on English in the Liturgy, ed., Collegeville, Minn.: The Liturgical Press, 1982, (hereafter DOL) 1, no. 106. See also ibid., Appendix, Declaration of the Second Vatican Ecumenical Council on Revision of the Calendar: DOL 1, no. 131.
2. See *Directory*, no. 8; see SC, art. 106: DOL 1, no. 106.
3. See *Directory*, no. 12.
4. See Paul VI, Address to bishops of central France, (26 March 1977): AAS 69 (1977), 465; "The goal must always be the celebration of the sacrifice of the Mass, the only true actualization of the Lord's paschal mystery" (DOL 449, no. 38:2).
5. See SC, art. 106: DOL 1, no. 106.
6. See *Directory*, no. 15.
7. Ibid., no. 2; see *Codex Iuris Canonici*, 1983 (hereafter, CIC), can. 1248, §2.
8. Ibid., no. 5.
9. Ibid., no. 6
10. Ibid., no. 32; see CIC, can. 1248, §2.
11. Ibid., no. 18.

12. See Paul VI, Address to bishops of Central France, (26 March 1977): AAS 69 (1977); "Proceed judiciously, but without multiplying this type of Sunday assembly, as though it were the ideal solution and the last chance" (DOL 449, no. 3842).

13. See *Directory*, no. 21.

14. Ibid., no. 22.

15. Ibid., no. 23.

16. Ibid., no. 24.

17. Ibid., no. 25; see SC Rites, Instruction *Eucharisticum mysterium* (25 May 1967), no. 26: AAS 59 (1967), 555; DOL 179, no. 1255.

18. Ibid., no. 25.

19. Ibid., no. 26.

20. Ibid., no. 27.

21. Ibid., no. 29; See Paul VI, Motu proprio *Ad pascendum* (15 August 1972), no. 1: AAS 64 (1972), 534; DOL 319, no. 2576.

22. Ibid., no. 38.

23. Ibid., no. 40.

24. Ibid., no. 40.

25. See *The Roman Ritual, Book of Blessings*, Part VI, Chapter 60.

26. See *Directory*, no. 30.

27. Ibid., no. 27; see CIC, can. 230, §3.

28. See SC, art. 28: DOL 1, no. 28.

29. See *Directory*, no. 31; see SC, art. 29: DOL 1, no. 29.

30. Ibid., no. 39; see *General Instruction of the Liturgy of the Hours* (hereafter GILH), no. 258: DOL 426, no. 3688; see also *The Roman Ritual, Book of Blessings*, nos. 48, 119, 130, 181.

31. See *The Roman Ritual, Holy Communion and Worship of the Eucharist outside Mass* (hereafter HCWEOM), no. 20: DOL 266, no. 2098.

32. "He or she does not use the presidential chair, but another chair prepared outside the sanctuary" (*Directory*, no. 40). See also GILH, no. 258: DOL 426, no. 3688.

33. See *Directory*, no. 40.

34. Ibid., no. 19.

35. SC, no. 7: DOL 1, no. 7.

36. See *The Liturgy of the Hours* (hereafter LOTH), New York: The Catholic Book Publishing Company, 1975-1976.

37. GILH, no. 22: DOL 426, no. 3452.

38. See *Directory*, no. 33.

39. See LOTH.

40. Ibid.

41. See SC, art. 35, 4: DOL 1, no. 35.

42. See HCWEOM, no. 26.

43. See *Directory*, no. 20.

44. Ibid., no. 40.

45. Ibid., no. 36.

46. See *The Roman Missal (Sacramentary)*.

47. See *Lectionary for Mass*, New York: The Catholic Book Publishing Company, 1970.

48. See *Directory*, no. 41.

49. Ibid., no. 42.
50. See CIC, can. 766-767.
51. See *Directory*, no. 43.
52. See GIRM, nos. 45-47: DOL 208, nos. 1435-1437.
53. Ibid., no. 44.
54. Ibid., no. 45.
55. See HCWEOM, ch. 1: DOL 266, nos. 2092-2103.
56. See *Directory*, no. 46.
57. Ibid., no. 28.
58. Ibid., no. 47.
59. Letter from the Congregation for Divine Worship and the Discipline of the Sacraments, (24 April 1991), Prot. N. CD 6/90.
60. See HCWEOM, no. 37.
61. *Directory*, no. 49.
62. See HCWEOM, no. 19: DOL 266, no. 2097.
63. Ibid., no. 37

OUTLINES OF THE RITES

MORNING PRAYER
[WITH HOLY COMMUNION]

Introductory Rites
  Introduction
  Hymn

Psalmody
  Antiphon 1
  Psalm
  [Psalm-prayer]
  Antiphon 2
  Old Testament Canticle
  Antiphon 3
  Psalm
  [Psalm-prayer]

Liturgy of the Word
  First Reading
  Responsorial Psalm
  Second Reading
  Gospel Acclamation
  Gospel
  Homily or Reflection
    on the Readings

Response to the Word of God
  (Responsory)
[Dismissal of the
  Catechumens]
Canticle of Zechariah
Intercessions

Lord's Prayer or
** Communion Rite**
  Sign of Peace
  Invitation to Communion
  Communion
  Concluding Prayer
  Prayer after Communion

Concluding Rite
  Brief Announcements
  [Collection of the
  Monetary Offerings of the
    Assembly]
  Blessing
  Dismissal

EVENING PRAYER
[WITH HOLY COMMUNION]

Introductory Rites
Introduction
Hymn

Psalmody
Antiphon 1
Psalm
[Psalm-prayer]
Antiphon 2
Psalm
[Psalm-prayer]
Antiphon 3
New Testament Canticle

Liturgy of the Word
First Reading
Responsorial Psalm
Second Reading
Gospel Acclamation
Gospel
Homily or Reflection
on the Readings

Response to the Word of God
(Responsory)
[Dismissal of the Catechumens]
Canticle of Mary
Intercessions

Lord's Prayer or
Communion Rite
Sign of Peace
Invitation to Communion
Communion
Concluding Prayer
Prayer after Communion

Concluding Rite
Brief Announcements
[Collection of the
Monetary Offerings of the
Assembly]
Blessing
Dismissal

CELEBRATION OF THE
LITURGY OF THE WORD
[WITH HOLY COMMUNION]

Introductory Rites
Greeting
Introduction
Litany in Praise of God's
    Mercy
Opening Prayer

Liturgy of the Word
First Reading
Responsorial Psalm
Second Reading
Gospel Acclamation
Gospel
Homily or Reflection
    on the Readings
[Dismissal of the
    Catechumens]

Profession of Faith
General Intercessions
Act of Thanksgiving

Lord's Prayer or
    Communion Rite
Sign of Peace
Invitation to Communion
Communion
Prayer after Communion

Concluding Rite
Brief Announcements
[Collection of the Monetary
    Offerings of the Assembly]
Blessing
Dismissal